A TOUR OF EAST ANTRIM

D0552621

In memory of my father, William Luney.

This book has received financial assistance under the
Cultural Traditions Programme which aims to encourage
acceptance and understanding of cultural diversity.

Friar's Bush Press
24 College Park Avenue
BELFAST BT7 ILR
Published 1990

ISBN O 946872 38 4

Designed by Rodney Miller Associates, Belfast.
Printed by W. & G. Baird, Antrim

The Photographs
Front cover: The Gobbins Hotel, Ballycarry (WAG 1474)
Back cover: Glynn Village (WAG 389)

The WAG numbers after each photograph refer to the
Green Collection held at the Ulster Folk and Transport
Museum, Cultra, Co. Down, from where prints may be
obtained.

A TOUR OF
East Antrim

Historic photographs from the
W. A. Green Collection
in the Ulster Folk and
Transport Museum.

Doreen Corcoran

Friar's Bush Press

Map of East Antrim, 1902, from *A Guide To Belfast and the Counties of Down and Antrim,* prepared for the meeting of the British Association by the Belfast Naturalists' Field Club (Belfast, 1902).

INTRODUCTION

William Alfred Green (1870-1958), who took the photographs on the following pages, was intended for a career in the family tea business. Poor health, however, forced him to find an occupation which would take him outdoors, and he became an apprentice assistant to R. J. Welch who was already established as the leading photographer in Ulster. Following the experimental years of the nineteenth century, photography had grown rapidly as a business and as a hobby. In 1881 there were 74 professional photographers in Ulster and thirty years later when Green went into business on his own account the number had reached 223.

After moving to Antrim he was drawn to observing country life and customs possibly because of their strangeness to a middle class townsman. In 1900 75% of the farms in the north were less than 30 acres and Green's attention to this basic but unremarked stratum of life here, between 1910 and 1930, has left compassionate and accurate glimpses of a past world of weary toil in all weathers relieved by close companionship and simple pleasures. Writing of the noted Welch collection, Professor Estyn Evans said that *'the only comparable collection of photographs by a serious student of folklife is that of Green (housed in the Ulster Folk and Transport Museum)'*, although he felt that Welch was the superior craftsman.

The photographs chosen for a *Tour of East Antrim* are not representative of Green's interest in rural life but demonstrate equally his curiosity and power of observation. The towns visited have little in common except proximity and the fact that, when visited by Green in the first quarter of this century, they were all lively centres of human activity. Larne with its splendid new cross-channel steamers, Whitehead appearing overnight as a stylish resort, Carrick steeped in a military past, and Ballyclare cannily going about its own business as always. Only Islandmagee hints at Green's special interest particularly in one photograph of a farmer showing off his wheelcar; those of the natural wonders of the Gobbins cliffs and the studies of field monuments are in keeping with current amateur enthusiasm at that time, which Green shared.

It should be remembered that Green was not a gentleman of leisure, passing time pleasantly by observing life around him. He was a working photographer in a competitive business, using his skill to keep his family in respectable comfort. Many of the photographs seen here were intended for reproduction as postcards by the established publishers. Some, shown in this book, were hand coloured and sold in packets under his own name. One such packet containing twelve postcards of Whitehead and labelled "Wagtail Series — W. A. Green, Publisher, Belfast" appears crudely finished in lurid colours compared with the excellence of modern colour photography, but has historical interest in itself as a stage towards that excellence.

This corner of Ireland was fortunate in having a sympathetic and competent observer at a specially interesting period when cameras and cars were only part of many fundamental changes in life here.

LARNE

Inver an Latharna - the river mouth in the land of Lathar.
The sight of land only twenty miles away across the channel attracted early man to this coast in the Stone Age and place names of later Celtic origin relate to forts and religious sites in the Iron Ages. Later still, the natural harbour was used by the Vikings whose name for the lough, Ulfreck's Fiord, survives in Olderfleet.

Edward Bruce landed here with his army in 1315 when he made a bid for the kingship of Ireland and in the unsettled years of the sixteenth and seventeenth centuries military control changed hands several times. Heavy settlement by Presbyterians from the Scottish lowlands produced in later years a homogeneous population of industrious and independent minded farmers and tradesmen.

The natural resources of plentiful water and good land brought increased wealth and population in the nineteenth century and the hinterland needed the port to channel products for export and to supply raw materials. Parallel with the industrial exploitation of the area was the recognition of its attractive coastline with safe bathing, sheltered recreation and a coastal panorama stretching to Scotland. At the time these photographs were taken the train which took businessmen to Belfast in 55 minutes brought back city folk looking for relief from the crowded houses, harsh factory conditions and fume-laden air. They could dress in fashionable clothes, dine in public and generally pretend for a short time that they lived in a more gracious world.

This happy picture of busy industry and organised leisure was replaced briefly on 25th April 1914 by a scene from John Buchan when Major Frederick Crawford landed 26,000 rifles and 3 million rounds of ammunition to oppose Home Rule. The operation took place in total secrecy, with local recruits cutting telephone wires. The arms were dispersed to private cars from a coal boat called the *Clyde Valley* but renamed *Mountjoy II* for the occasion.

This was also the reign of the extraordinary Amanda McKittrick Ros who imagined that her romantic extravaganzas in novel and verse were lauded in the London salons and wrote to a friend on one occasion 'I expect I will be talked about in a thousand years.' Despite being mundanely married to Andrew Ross, station master at Larne Harbour, she saw herself as a literary lion and like William MacGonigal never realised that the popular success of her writing lay in the amused disbelief of the reading public. Literary critics joined in the joke with mock reviews and she responded *'I afford pleasure and give satisfaction to the million and one who continually thirst for aught that drops from my pen.'*

Passengers and freight traffic through Larne reached a peak during the Second World War with the movement of troops and war supplies. Local people hardened in the tradition of sea faring were amused by the terrifying reputation which the route acquired among the thousands of men arriving to train for service overseas. The confluence of several currents and resultant violent gales can produce a rough passage for those not used to the sea. This reputation sadly, became reality in 1953 when exceptional seas disabled the ferry *Princess Victoria* which sank with a loss of 136 lives.

In recent years the town has suffered economic uncertainty but the port continues successfully, though changing in style with the increase in containers and the disappearance of rail passengers. The promenaders have deserted to the Mediterranean.

LARNE, *c.* 1915 (WAG 527)

The railway line from Belfast reached Larne in 1862 and at its peak in the 1940s, forty-one passenger trains ran each way every day with engines named after local castles. Freight was carried in long lines of wagons filled with bread, coal, cows, etc. The station has since been moved, in very reduced form, to the reclaimed land of the bay, and the site of the engine sheds with the marketyard behind, is occupied by a new road system. The tower of the Town Hall pin-points Main Street. The houses in the foreground are Jubilee Row on the Shore Road, built just before 1900.

MAIN STREET, LARNE *c.* 1915 (WAG 528)
Reference was made in the nineteenth century to the 'old town' as near-derelict and the 'new town' consisting of one long new street with fine dwellings and business premises. This became Main Street and the spine of the present town. The Town Hall is just out of sight on the left and part of the old Court House is on the right (with cleaner's notice). The bank next door is now a housing office and the Railway Bar further along is now Craigs Cellars.

MAIN STREET - McNEILL'S HOTEL, *c.* 1915 (WAG 529)

Henry McNeill, popularly known as 'Knock-'em-down' had a flair for attracting and organising visitors in large numbers, in a way which foreshadowed modern tourism. His business was first established in 1853 and within ten years he had a fleet of horsedrawn cars and waggonettes for *'Excursions, Pic-nic and Tourist parties'* which were *'conducted to any point in the County* *Antrim and with Luncheons etc'* (G. H. Bassett, *County Antrim one hundred years ago).* This was originally the Central Refreshment Rooms and the handsome frontage shown here (still standing though derelict) was erected in 1910 after a fire. The tariff around 1910 was 4/- per day or one guinea per week.

CROSS STREET, LARNE *c.* 1915 (WAG 546)

The tower of the Town Hall marks Main Street, dividing Upper and Lower Cross Street. Charles McGarel of Magheramorne built the Town Hall in 1869 *'for the use of the people for ever.'* It contained a public hall, library and museum. The wall in the distance has steps which led to the Fair Hill now obliterated by a new road system. Halliday Brothers' fine store had grocery and hardware departments and also sold toys, postcards and stationery.

DUNLUCE STREET, *c.* 1915 (WAG 547)

Looking towards Cross Street with Halliday Brothers' building in the distance. Today's street seems dull compared with this lively picture of busy shops and customers, goods on display and bicycles and vehicles. Bassett's guide (1888) lists six grocers in this street with eight other tradesmen or businesses. A draper advertised *'the latest London and Paris Fashions in every Department.'*

BARNHILL AND MAIN STREET, LARNE, *c.* 1915 (WAG 544)
The Methodist church beside Barnhill Terrace was designed by
S. P. Close and built in 1884. The large block behind is one end of
the Laharna Hotel whose package tours were so popular that
another storey was added later (£2-7-6 for one week's board,
residence and daily excursions). The owner William Holden had
saloon carriages and wagon-lit style dining cars specially fitted in
Belfast for his railway tours.

CURRAN ROAD, *c.* 1915 (WAG 530)
Barnhill Terrace is now on the left. The Electric Theatre had just been opened by Irish Electric Theatres Ltd. There was a matinee showing at 3.00 p.m., continuous performance from 6.30 p.m. and a complete change of programme every Monday and Thursday, seats 3d., 6d., and 1/-. This was replaced in 1936 by the Regal Cinema (seating 1,000). The R.I.C. Barracks was on the right side of this road which led directly from Main Street to the harbour.

OLDERFLEET HOTEL, LARNE, *c.* 1915 (WAG 533)

The hotel was built by James Chaine in 1878 as part of his ambitious plans to improve the harbour. It boasted a ladies' drawingroom and reading and billiard rooms and was described in 1888 in Bassett's guide, as *'beautifully situated . . . combined railway and hotel tickets issued at Belfast and Ballymena.'* The harbour station is on the right and Lord Randolph Churchill is reported as dining here with the station master, Andy Ross, on his visits to Belfast. The fishing yawls drawn up on the shore have gone and the hotel is now marooned in a huge car and lorry park for the ferry.

STRANRAER FERRY, *c.* 1925 (WAG 2564)

In 1846 Capt. George Adams, R.N., reported to the admiralty that Larne offered the safest and easiest access in the north. When James Chaine bought the harbour in 1865 he devoted his considerable energies to promoting the cross-channel route and exploiting the natural assets of the area. He built a new jetty in 1871, persuaded American steamers to call, and obtained Queen Victoria's permission to name his new ferries after her daughters. The ship leaving the harbour is the second Princess Victoria built by Wm Denny and Son, Dumbarton, and launched in 1912. The merchant vessel on the left is the *Phyllis Seed* built in 1908 and registered in Liverpool.

THE CURRAN (WAG 2563)

It is quite clear why the gravel spit stretching one mile from the harbour into Larne Lough was called in Irish *coran* - a sickle. The Curran, geologically, is a raised beach, described by *The Shell Guide to Ireland* as *'one of the most remarkable prehistoric stations in these islands'* on account of the enormous quantity of Mesolithic flint found there. The arrival here of Edward Bruce in 1315 with 300 ships must have been an awesome sight. A happier assembly was the first regatta in 1887 of the Corinthian Sailing Club.

OLDERFLEET CASTLE, *c*.1915 (WAG 534)
The scant remains of a castle which once commanded the
anchorage from the middle of the Curran. The site was fortified
from the twelfth century and an English captain is recorded here
in 1542 with a galley to keep the sea clear of Redshanks (Highland
Scots). Sir Moyses Hill improved the defences on being made
Governor of Olderfleet in 1569. The ruins reveal a four storey
fortified tower with gun loops in each side and traces of a bastion.
The cottage on the right was a coastguard station.

GENTLEMEN'S BATHING PLACE, LARNE, *c.* 1915 (WAG 537)
A committee of residents met in 1885 to consider improvements including bathing places for both sexes. Boxes were one penny or one shilling and sixpence per month. This was a pleasant stroll from the harbour, past the park on the Bank Heads on the left, to the cliff path which joined the Coast Road in the distance. Appropriately, the modern indoor Tower Pool was built opposite the changing rooms shown here, which can still be seen with the stone steps and base of the diving platform.

DRUMALIS, *c.* 1915 (WAG 550)

The high ground overlooking the promenade was a traditional gathering place at set festivals, and several buildings have occupied the site over the centuries. This house was designed by S. P. Close for Sir Hugh Smiley, Bart., in 1872 and acquired by a religious order in 1930 for a retreat. The very beautiful panelling, stained glass and marble fireplaces remain in situ. In the gun running episode in 1914 the widowed Lady Smiley allowed local men to assemble on the lawns to be marshalled into units and given instructions.

BANK HEADS, LARNE, *c.* 1915 (WAG 539)

The Town Park still occupies this vantage point overlooking the promenade and the entrance to Larne Lough although it is no longer true that *'in the morning the scene is enhanced by the merry business of the bathers on the beach below.'* G. H. Bassett writing in 1888 continues, *'upon these verdant slopes the summer population* *delight to recline and divide time between the view of rocks, sea and sky and the consumption of light literature'* — and (later) ice-cream, as indicated by the cart which can just be seen in the foreground. The view now unfortunately includes the three chimneys of Ballylumford Power Station on the opposite shore.

CHAINE MEMORIAL TOWER, (WAG 536)
Local legend maintains that James Chaine was buried upright in
this tower. His unusual resting place is actually within an Iron
Age promontory fort on the Bank Heads overlooking this spot
and the simple inscription reads *'Private burying ground of James
Chaine, Esq., M.P. of Cairncastle Lodge.'* He died in 1885, aged only
44 years and the tower (92 feet high in Annalong granite) was
designed by S. P. Close and erected by public subscription in
1887. Fittingly the top has navigation lights for ships entering the
harbour.

CLIFF PATH AT WATERLOO, LARNE c. 1915 (WAG 540)
This is the furthest stretch of the walk which began at the harbour and is little changed today, though wider and better surfaced. The area takes its name from Waterloo Cottage built in the year of the battle and the fort containing the Chaine grave is high above the path at this point. There is a lime kiln further along where the way divides, left onto the Coast Road behind the houses and right to Pebble Cottage.

BLACK CAVE TUNNEL (WAG 2191)

Charles Lanyon, the county surveyor encouraged the idea of a Coast Road, and a Scottish engineer, William Bald, finished the difficult construction in 1842. Parts of the road made use of the raised beach but much blasting was necessary, as here, to tunnel through solid rock. Tourist traffic to the Glens and beyond grew rapidly after this date. The Black Cave, 60 feet long was a local attraction, as was the Devil's Churn beyond the rocks shown here. A boulder memorial and plaque to William Bald was placed here in 1979.

GLENO FROM EAST (WAG 2973)
This hamlet is perched on the edge of a limestone cliff overlooking the valley of the Glynn river and at one time was on the route from Carrickfergus to Larne. Its position now, off the beaten track, makes a quiet refuge for those who can find it. The steep brae and narrow corner on the road from Carrickfergus (where a child leans on the wall) are more hazardous for the car driver than the leisurely horse and laden sidecar.

GLENO FROM WEST (WAG 1099)
The name Gleno probably means *'the glen of the cave'* and although the glens of Antrim are further north, this valley has the same character in miniature, with cottages clinging to the slope and the deep glen and waterfall unexpectedly dropping away behind the street.

WATERFALL AT GLENO (WAG 302)

Above the village the Glynn river has four cascades within a short distance, the last being a cutting 50 feet high. The banks are carpeted with ivy, and mosses and ferns of many varieties flourish in the damp shade of mature beeches. The glen and falls were given to the National Trust in 1968. The Trust has renewed the steps and bridge and planted more trees.

BRAES OF GLYNN (WAG 2195)

This pleasant sweep of land between Glynn and Larne is still very attractive despite the industrial outlook across the lough. The old Gleno road has splendid views from the height above at Ardmore. The Shore Road follows the foot of the slope and crosses the railway coming from Glynn station on the right. This is a rewarding area for watching birds, especially waterfowl which breed safely in stretches of water, as here, cut off by the railway embankment.

GLYNN, MAIN STREET, *c.*1910 (WAG 390)
Glynn was such a charming rural village with well maintained thatched cottages that it made an ideal film set for Richard Hayward and his company to make the popular 'Luck of the Irish' in 1935. This caused such interest that a policeman had to be fetched from Larne to control the crowd.

GLYNN RIVER AND BRIDGE, *c.*1910 (WAG 391)

Heavy traffic for Larne Harbour has been diverted to a new road and the village can slumber on, without the thatch. Trains still stop at the station beyond the beeches on left. The lade coming through the right hand arch of the lovely old bridge is no longer needed to channel the water which turned the wheel of John Hawthorne's corn mill on the other side of the road. The village used to be known for its whitening mill (using the fine chalk found here) and also for the strange wooden scizzors used for pulling thistles, produced by a wood-turner in the saw-mill.

WHITEHEAD

Whitehead in the early nineteenth century was a clachan of cottages on a steep incline overlooking the sea on the Carrickfergus side of the promontory of that name. When the railway was extended from Carrick to Larne in 1862 a halt was made on that exposed side of the tunnel carrying the line through the headland. After protests by local people a platform was built on the sheltered side of the tunnel in 1863.

On that side, the bay between the limestone White Head and the basalt Black Head contained only the ruined Castle Chichester and a coastguard station and even in 1888 Bassett's guide records only a sub post office and 15 farms. However, the opportunity provided by the railway and the potential attraction of the scenic setting with safe bathing and boating were soon realised. Amenities for holiday-makers - promenade, bandstand and bathing boxes - and the introduction of a 'villa ticket' giving new householders free travel to Belfast for ten years, brought rapid growth of housing and accompanying business.

An extra long excursion platform was added to the station in 1907 and for the next 50 years in this *'Eden of Ulster'* (as described by a guide book of the time) the summer months filled the hotels and guest houses and day trippers thronged the sea front. Scottish accents predominated, particularly during the Glasgow Fair Fortnight and many came faithfully every year. The deeds of a house built just before 1900 give the address as Marine Parade, Chichester-on-sea which, although overtaken by the common use of Whitehead suggests stylish bustles and debonair straw boaters.

The river divided the land of the Dobbs family and that of Lord Donegall, and building had been limited by the latter's reluctance to allow change. His young successor was of a different mind and today the houses of the second phase, in the twenties and thirties are distinct from the earlier Edwardian town. The Urban District Council proudly provided a swimming pool in 1931, added bowling and putting greens and attracted a cinema. The railway contributed to this change by lifting the surface of wooden sleepers on the promenade and replacing them with concrete. However, despite success, the resort always had a genteel air and although keen to attract business, never encouraged the comic postcard image.

A remarkable resident at this time was Charlotte Despard, a sister of Field Marshal Sir John French, Viceroy of Ireland. She liked to be known as Madame Despard but locals preferred Madame Despert and regarded her with mixed awe and suspicion as she swept around the town in a 14 horse power Lanchester, wearing a mantilla. She had become famous in London as a suffragette and in her eighties built a square white flat-roofed house (looking like a stray from Hollywood) on the cliff overlooking the promenade in 1935.

Changing fashion and cheap continental travel have left Whitehead as a pleasant residential town with the yachts still bobbing at anchor in the summer and the path to Black Head now busy with doggy walkers. The seascape from the lighthouse does not change. The view takes the eye from the Paps of Jura (on a really lucky day) past Kintyre and Ailsa Craig, a glimpse of the Isle of Man on to the Copelands and Helen's Tower in Belfast Lough with Scrabo beyond. It is not a mirage: it is Whitehead.

WHITEHEAD BEFORE 1920 (WAG 775)

This bird's eye view from White Head to Black Head shows the first development of the early l900s. A railway siding for the quarry runs from the shed at the right, to join the main line as it leaves the shore to enter the station. The coastguard station is in the foreground with its boat-house (given an arch under the railway line) across the road, and the Gentlemen's Bathing Place on the shore. The white painted yacht club marks the beginning of the promenade with the bandstand and white marquee at the other end.

RAILWAY STATION, WHITEHEAD *c.* 1928 (WAG 757)

In 1864 the first station here was one platform with an old carriage used as a waiting room and a single line. The present station was complete by 1900 and a long excursion platform on the other side (now used by the Railway Preservation Society of Ireland) was built in 1907. The footbridge in the distance gives access to the beach from Cable Road. The station footbridge from which this photograph was taken has since been dismantled. Following protests by the Women's Temperance League in 1883 the refreshment room had to offer tea as well as alcohol and close after the last train.

VICTORIA AVENUE, *c.* 1920 (WAG 1086)

As the name implies, this was an early road which came into being following the building of the station at this end. St Patrick's Church of Ireland church was erected in 1908 and Our Lady of Lourdes Roman Catholic church at the top of the hill in 1909. The Earlswood Hotel on the left became the Royal Hotel in the 1930s and its owner Mr Devenny advertised in the town guide, a *'400 mile tour in de luxe safety saloon coaches'* to the Glens of Antrim and the Mourne Mountains. Seven days accommodation with all meals cost f4.10.0; without tours it cost £2.15.0 . Supplies for these meals can be seen in the foreground.

CHESTER AVENUE, WHITEHEAD, *c.* 1915 (WAG 756)
This is the approach to the station on the seaward side. The Whitehead Hotel was a subsidiary of the Albert Hotel in Belfast and has since become the Whitecliff. Marine Avenue opposite, led to the promenade and the open foreground has become the Fire Station. The Tower Cafe on the right has reverted to a private residence, the fate of many guest houses when the holiday business deserted the town.

CABLE ROAD, *c*. 1912 (WAG 761)

Formerly Queen's Avenue, with King's Avenue on the left, followed by Balmoral and Victoria Avenues. The telegraph cable link with Britain was laid in 1893 (via Portpatrick) and the line is marked by the lozenge-topped pole. Another can be seen in the distance at the cable station beside the yacht club. The cable was removed in 1951. The provision merchant remains under a different name but with the fancy coloured glass windows intact.

YACHT CLUB AND PROMENADE, WHITEHEAD (WAG 755)
A small boat club was replaced by this building in 1911 which became the headquarters of the Co. Antrim Yacht Club and home of the Waveney class. The footbridge from Cable Road is on the left, with the station footbridge in the distance. The houses in Marine Parade beyond, were built before 1900, the earliest in the town. Here, the summer season is under way with the marquee erected at the bandstand and the promenade busy with visitors.

PROMENADE FROM THE BANKS, LATE 1920s (WAG 2220)
The promenade was laid out in 1900 with seats and an open-sided bandstand. The slope was terraced with wooden seating under the marquee. There were several performances daily of Pierrot and Vaudeville shows. The boxes for the Ladies Bathing Place can be seen on the shore with the ivy covered Castle Chichester behind the buildings opposite. Sand was carted from Portrush to improve the beach and retained by the railway sleepers, seen here, as breakwaters.

COASTGUARD STATION, WHITEHEAD (WAG 769)
The Ordnance Survey Memoirs (1839) record a chief boatman and five coastguards here. There were three stations in Islandmagee and two in Larne which indicate the extent of water borne traffic around the peninsula before modern roads - and the amount of smuggling expected. The early station was in cottages on the shore and replaced by this impressive block in 1850 (now converted to private dwellings.)

CASTLE CHICHESTER (WAG 767)

The soldier adventurer Sir Moyses Hill came to Ireland in 1573 and obtained a lease of Islandmagee. He built this tower house at the south end in 1604 and named it after his patron Sir Arthur Chichester. Residence must have been brief, as Richard Dobbs describes it in 1683 without a roof. For the following two centuries the area was known as Castle Chichester and it was a strange fate for the ruined shell, to be surrounded by the guest houses and ice cream parlours of the new town of Whitehead.

PROMENADE LOOKING TOWARDS WHITE HEAD, *c.* 1915
(WAG 1089)

Marine Avenue brought visitors directly from the station into the middle of the promenade. Marine Hotel on the corner (with porch) was in business as early as 1897. P. Bonugli, whose sign can be seen on the right was one of several Italian families who came to Glasgow from Barga in Tuscany, and followed the Scottish holiday-makers to the east Antrim resorts. The railway line and tunnel through the headland are in the distance on the left.

PROMENADE LOOKING TOWARDS BLACK HEAD, *c.* 1915
(WAG 1088)

The landing stage in the background was constructed in 1900 at the same time as the promenade and boat trips to Black Head or to Bangor were part of the seaside experience along with 'dips' and sand castles. The railway sleepers used for surfacing are clearly seen here and lasted until 1935. The Ladies Bathing Place, behind the interested spectators, was replaced by an out-door swimming pool in 1931. Has the boy on the left stolen his sister's straw hat?

GENTLEMEN'S BATHING PLACE, WHITEHEAD WAG 753)

Sea bathing became a fashionable health fad of the gentry in the eighteenth century. By 1900 enjoyment rather than endurance was the key note but the sexes were still strictly segregated as men could expose arms and legs while women still wore frilled smocks and pantaloons. The men here were relegated to the south end of the sea front, beyond the promenade and yacht club. The narrow gangway along the railway embankment ruled out peeping women and the railing made a useful clothes line. This all disappeared in 1928 when a second railway line was built around the headland.

RECREATION GROUNDS, c. 1915 (WAG 764)

The daily shows, trips from the landing stage (see boats lying behind the bandstand) and the popular Kennedy's cafe made this the jolly end of the promenade. Kennedy's first opened for business in 1885, was rebuilt after a fire and remained a favourite gathering spot for many years. This is still a recreation area with tables and seats, but no longer any organised entertainments and the boats are on dry land on the parking lot made by surfacing the shingled point on the right.

BLACK HEAD, PATH AND PORT DAVEY (WAG 2019)

William Valentine, a director of the railway company suggested a path to Black Head in 1881 and by 1888 a walk of one and a quarter miles had been laid out with seats and a shelter (shown here). This was later extended north to join the Gobbins path. Port Davey had been an early mail packet station for Scotland. The house in the centre belonged to the Hoy family for many generations and was recently destroyed by fire. The two erratic boulders on the shore are the Wren's Eggs.

BLACK HEAD AND SUNSHINE HOUSE (WAG 762)

The path continued around the foot of the headland (see metal bridge), reached the lighthouse by steps and returned on the slopes to the left of the hotel. The view stretches from Kintyre to Belfast. The earliest lighthouse had burnt coal for illumination in the seventeenth century. The present light and keepers' houses were built in 1902. The board for Sunshine House proclaims a Temperance Hotel and Tearooms, opened in 1901 by James Wylie, designer of the Waverley class racing yacht. A contemporary guide book advertisement described the premises *'surrounded by a charming amphitheatre of bold headlands which form a shelter.'*

MULDERSLEIGH AND BLACK HEAD (WAG 1464)
Although now a peninsula, the character of Islandmagee remains that of an island - self sufficient, proud and clannish. It is an old saying that if someone is kicked, the whole island goes lame. Their capacity for spending their lives at sea and yet remaining rooted in the land led Jack London to describe them in *The Strength of the strong* as sea farmers. The population at the turn of the century doubled during the summer months and many wooden bungalows built then to accommodate visitors are still in use.

CLOUGHFIN (WAG 2959)

The name, meaning *'white stone'* probably refers to the plentiful limestone and one of the island's twenty lime kilns was worked here. The cottage is typical of the island at that time and this scene has scarcely changed today except that there are no longer the summer activities. The cove (beyond the wall) had a bathing place with a springboard and an annual regatta. In addition to sailing and rowing events there was fancy dress, greasy pole competitions and a local band playing all day.

GOBBINS HOTEL, BALLYCARRY (WAG 1474)

A popular outing was a train ride to Ballycarry station where according to a notice in a guide dated 1906 *'the following car owners meet the trains and will be pleased to accommodate tourists or others who may wish their services at Moderate charges to the Gobbins or elsewhere'* and a choice of 8 names was offered. The charge from the station to the Gobbins and back was 3s for four people. The energetic could walk there in one and a quarter hours following the finger post at Sammy Duff's loanin down to Busby's cottage. Refreshment could be enjoyed here while waiting for the return train (the station entrance is opposite the hotel).

HILLSPORT AND THE GOBBINS (WAG 2023)

The port was named after the Hill family who farmed the land. Lime from the kiln (behind the house) was shipped to Scotland. The path to Black Head was extended to join the route around the Gobbins and here walkers could rest and have tea. This profile of the cliffs possibly explains the name which usually means *'mouth'* in Irish but is more likely to be *'snout'* in this *case*.

WISE'S EYE, THE GOBBINS c. 1910 (WAG 521)
The coast on the south side of Islandmagee was known to geologists and naturalists, and well-to-do families used to drive from Belfast in their carriages to picnic on the cliffs, but access to the spectacular rock formations below was difficult and dangerous. The Northern Counties Railway was keen to attract passengers and in 1892 their chief engineer, Berkeley Dean Wise began surveying a possible path, tunnelling where necessary and using metal bridges to span gaps.

THE SANDY CAVE, THE GOBBINS, 1910 (WAG 517)
The exciting enterprise was opened in time for the meeting in Belfast of the British Association for the Advancement of Science in 1902. According to William J. Fennell, Vice-President of the Belfast Naturalists Field Club, *'The Directors claimed the privilege of acting as hosts to the visitors'* and on 20th August a special train took delegates to see the natural and man-made wonders. The tables above suggest refreshments but the photographer has arrived before the supplies.

TUBULAR BRIDGE AND MAN O' WAR SEA STACK, THE
GOBBINS, 1910 (WAG 516)
The Man O' War is seventy feet high and was named by local
boatmen used to seeing its striking outline from the sea. The
metal bridges were made and assembled in the shipyard in Belfast
and floated down the lough on barges to be installed. The cliffs
reach 290 feet at the highest point and the water at 19 fathoms
deep adds to the viewer's awe, though not to the nonchalant man
on the bridge.

THE SWINGING BRIDGE, 1910 (WAG 524)

Severe gales in March and April each year twisted the metal work, caused rock falls and meant expensive annual repairs before the summer season. So much damage was sustained during the wartime closure from 1940-1951 (due to lack of staff) that the railway could not afford a major rebuilding and the path finally closed in 1961. Bird watchers are still attracted there by boat especially to see one of Ireland's few puffin colonies.

COTTAGES ON THE GOBBINS ROAD, ISLANDMAGEE c.1910
(WAG 1475)
This photograph was entitled *'Islandmagee farmsteads on the road to the Gobbins'* but the uniform row of 3 cottages is not in the local tradition of lone single farm houses. These are more likely to be the coastguard station above Hillsport which closed before 1900 and the 3 houses became private dwellings although continuing to be known as Coastguards' Row.

PORT MUCK AND MUCK ISLAND (WAG 1463)

Muck (*muc*, a pig) refers to the shape of the island and is no reflection on local cleanliness. There are puzzling remnants of a castle keep, above McClelland's farm, overlooking the harbour. The jetty was built in 1827 when almost a hundred herring boats fished these waters and the house at the shore has a bay in the gable where harbour dues were paid. Horse's Cave on the island kept smuggled animals hidden while awaiting shipment. A famous hoax in 1812 brought people from as far as Belfast to see a mermaid said to have been caught in a net.

BROWN'S BAY, ISLANDMAGEE (WAG 951)

TO BE LET DURING THE BATHING SEASON

A neat cabin consisting of two compleat furnished Rooms, pleasantly situated on Brown's Bay, in Isle Magee . . . the bottom is white sand and the strength of the water is equal, if not superior, to most other places. NORTHERN STAR, 25th April 1796.

This advertisement is proof that the popularity of this bay was not a new discovery by the motor car. Happy diversions in the summer could be misleading as in the New Year 1867 when the square rigger *Berbice* foundered in the bay, with no survivors, during gales.

A WHEELCAR AT BROWN'S BAY, *c.*1910 (WAG 955)

Islandmagee had few big houses or one-room cabins, so this farm is typical of the stout stone dwellings of the farmers and artisans forming most of the population. The narrow lanes and damp conditions kept the traditional wheel-less slipe and slide car in use until about 1900. The farmer here, with a wheelcar and slate roof, would have been happy to show off for the camera. The flower-bed with whitewashed edges and Bess's upturned bucket add homely touches.

ROCKING STONE (WAG 956)

Erratics or large boulders deposited by the retreating Ice Age are common on this coast but their size has encouraged legends and superstitions about their magical properties and the giants who must have put them there. This example on the path at the eastern end of Brown's Bay is estimated to weigh ten to twelve tons and at this time could be swayed by pushing a particular spot with one finger. Following attempts to overturn it, a concrete bed now holds the stone secure but has removed some of the mystical aura.

DRUIDS' ALTAR (WAG 958)

The fanciful association with Druids' was common with early field monuments but this is undoubtedly a Neolithic chambered tomb set remarkably at the front door of an attractive Victorian villa. When visited by the historian Samuel McSkimin, the dolmen was in the garden of a cottage and his account in the *Dublin Penny* *Journal* (29 December 1832) with accompanying woodcut, describes six supporting uprights in two rows with a surrounding stone circle. Only three uprights with the surmounting capstone (six feet high) remain.

MILL BAY, ISLANDMAGEE (WAG 2164)

Before a corn mill was built in the eighteenth century this was Carnspindle Bay (from the charming original name Garryspinnel, a gooseberry garden). This is a pretty spot for a stroll along the lane, right, to the harbour which is derelict but eye catching with white limestone walls. The boathouse has been remodelled as a dwelling and the cottages unobtrusively modernised. The large building on the left was Jackson's Bar, the only survivor of fourteen public houses recorded on the island in 1839.

BARNEY'S POINT, *c.*1910 (WAG 3588)
The papers of both the Belfast Naturalists Field Club and the Belfast Natural History and Philosophical Society record frequent visits to the Antrim coast to examine geological phenomena. The well dressed ladies in bonnets self consciously searching for specimens are almost certainly in a party with the photographer and have arrived at Barney's *(bairneach* - a limpet) Point via Magheramorne railway station where a ferryboat crossed to Mill Bay one mile north of the point.

CARRICKFERGUS

When John de Courcy arrived in south Antrim in 1177 and built a formidable castle to establish military control of Ulster, there was no civil settlement at what is now Carrickfergus. The town grew quickly at the foot of the castle walls and in the mediaeval period, became a busy market and port, and eventually, the principal town in Ulster, although normal life was disrupted by periods of unrest when the English garrison came under attack.

The appointment of Sir Arthur Chichester as governor in 1603 marked a decline in Carrick's status. Despite building a mansion described by Sir William Brereton as *'like a prince's palace'* his plans for the new town of Belfast diverted his energies and gradually the authority of Carrick was usurped although the castle remained a major factor in Irish defence. By 1649 a Presbyterian minister Patrick Adair could refer admiringly to Belfast as *'the place where country gentlemen and officers most haunted'*. Professor Strahan's assertion that *'the history of the little city is the history of Ulster writ small'* no longer held true.

The uneasy resolution of religious conflict in 1690 left the English settlement secure within the walls and the Irish and Scots both seen as potentially disloyal, removed each night by the curfew bell at 9.00 p.m. The next century brought the shortlived excitement in 1756 of Thurot's occupation, when French manners charmed the ladies and the brief dashing appearance of John Paul Jones in the *Ranger* in 1778. John Wesley drew full houses on his seven visits and the Rev. Dr Beaufort wrote from the parlour of Mr Weir's inn of *'the respectable town'* of Carrickfergus. Samuel McSkimin settled in the town in 1797 and while earning his living as a grocer, applied intelligence and curiosity to compiling the *History and Antiquities of the County of the town of Carrickfergus*, which has gone into many editions.

The nineteenth century brought the industrial growth and improved communications experienced generally throughout Ireland. Railways and piped water convinced Victorians that they lived in a Golden Age and contemporary advertisements have a note of pride in a remarkable variety of products and services. Taylor's mill had its own school and fire brigade. Thirteen shipowners and 433 registered vessels used the harbour. An unexpected discovery in 1851 put packets of *CARRICK SALT* on every kitchen shelf in the kingdom. And still the castle loomed large with much of the commerce dependent on the maintenance of its fabric and personnel, and life was brightened by the spectacle and colour of uniforms and military ceremonial.

The early years of the century appear full of character, interest and liveliness with plays and dances, the regatta and the feis, and summer evenings when the entire population seemed to be strolling along the Scotch quarter looking for spaces on the sea wall to sit and survey the social scene. It must have appeared quite proper for the Royal yacht *Victoria and Albert* to be moored in the harbour on 22nd June 1921 when King George V and Queen Mary came to visit Belfast.

Two world wars brought Carrick into action again as a garrison town though the castle was an outmoded relic of another age. Thousands of troops on both occasions were quartered in tented encampments in the grounds of Sunnylands House. In the Great War the accents were all Irish but in 1940 the defeated Belgians came to restore their morale, and later well-dressed Americans stole all the girls while being trained for the front line.

The post war boom in artificial fabrics proved a chimera and after a few defeated years the town is putting on a new face hoping for success in smaller enterprises and in exploiting the reminders of the past. Brereton's *'preattie little town'* is recovering its pride.

CARRICKFERGUS FROM THE HARBOUR (WAG 1752)

The castle has dominated the town visually and materially for 800 years. There was no previous settlement here and although the town acquired importance in its own right its fortunes were affected constantly by the fortress in its midst. This townscape from the harbour entrance includes the pretty Gill's Almhouse on the left, a pleasing variety of buildings in Governor's Place (most still there) and the Boat Club (now a restaurant). The drawbridge on the right allowed cargo to be carried directly on and off carts. The shed at the castle, stored goods from cargo vessels for a local firm.

CARRICKFERGUS CASTLE (WAG 2557)

Few castles in Ireland have been continuously occupied from the twelfth century to the twentieth century which makes Carrick castle a picture book of varying military strategies and adaptations to counter improving weaponry. The visual drama of the near impregnable position on a dolerite dyke platform almost surrounded by sea has been lost in this aspect today by a car park on reclaimed land. The stylish steam yacht was a status symbol of the period and may have been built by John Hilditch in Carrick.

THE NORTH GATE, *c.* 1910 (WAG 103)

The walls of Carrick are not so celebrated as those of Derry but are earlier (1610). Larger carts of the Victorian era found passage through the gate difficult and a memorial asking for its removal was made to the Grand Jury in 1886. The restoration of 1911 to mark the accession of George V assured its survival and at present, lengths of wall on each side are being cleared to public view. The farrier's yard and hay loft hugging the wall on the left have gone. Mrs Smiley's home bakery on the right is being restored as part of the public access.

HIGH STREET, CARRICKFERGUS (WAG 1757)
The mediaeval street plan has remained almost intact. Market Place with Great Patrick (a large stone cross) was the focal point of the town and remained so, with the Big Lamp erected in 1881, especially on Saturday nights when appropriated by the Salvation Army for hymn singing. A replica has happily been installed in 1990 though without the 200 candle power of the original (or the bent upright). Bell's shop on left was a noted landmark and meeting place.

SHAFTESBURY PARK *c*.1920 (WAG 1760)
Harriet, daughter of the third Marquis of Donegall, married the eighth Earl of Shaftesbury. Her son and his countess paid a ceremonial visit to the town on 22nd March 1901 and later donated this land for a public park. The picture taken from the railway embankment shows the only expanse of the town wall visible to the public at that time. The back of the Presbyterian manse is on the left and the triple expanse of roof is the Army Ordnance Stores for which Carrick was the Head Depot.

JOYMOUNT AND SCOTCH QUARTER, CARRICKFERGUS
(WAG 1754)
Joymount Palace, named as a compliment to Lord Mountjoy, stood to the left of the picture and the eastern end of the town wall met the shore behind the crowd standing so obediently for the photographer. Although the Scottish settlers of the seventeenth century lived beyond the wall, a road was not built until 1770. Dobbs in 1683 writes *'the East Gate directs to the sea and is not to be rid out* [on horseback] *at full sea especially spring tides.'* The shore on the right is now buried under the Marine Gardens.

64

SCOTCH QUARTER (WAG 1755)

Dobbs' account continues that the Gate directs *'likewise to a small suburb called the Scotch Quarter. Here dwell the fishers and here lie the fishing boats belonging to the town.'* In succeeding centuries industry grew up behind the houses (note the chimney of the bleachworks) and pollution from both eventually destroyed the herring shoals and the oyster beds. The sea wall was a popular grandstand for superintending bathing and sandcastle building in the summer. A four lane highway now occupies the foreground.

GREEN STREET, CARRICKFERGUS, *c.*1920 (WAG 123)
The only recognisable feature here is the profile in the centre distance of the distinctive house overlooking the shore, built for himself by the noted architect S. P. Close. The row on the right was levelled for the Marine Highway although the long established Royal Oak public house (with large window) moved only to the other side of the road where the varied collection of buildings shown here had also disappeared. The name of the street does not refer to the photographer but possibly relates to the green used for drying the fishing nets.

EDEN, *c.*1920 (WAG 1756)
The present name has been shortened from Edengrenny meaning the sunny brow of the hill. Although less than 2 miles from Carrick, the village had an entirely separate identity and in earlier years faction fights occurred between the youths of Eden and those of the town. A planned modernisation scheme has rebuilt the street in traditional style houses so the overall appearance is unchanged despite the approaching suburbs of Carrick.

THE ROUND HOUSE, KILROOT (WAG 304)

Known locally as Dean Swift's house, this is more likely to date from the eighteenth century fashion for romantic cottages. Jonathan Swift was Prebendary of Kilroot 1695-6 and the strong local association may relate to an earlier house. The diminutive appearance is deceiving) as the ground floor contained a parlour twenty four feet by sixteen feet. The building was demolished in 1959 after a fire and the site and the adjacent Kilroot railway station have disappeared under the new power station.

WOODBURN — LOWER FALLS (WAG 1763)

The Woodburn river was *'the most remarkable both for its size and beauty; probably possessing as much natural and delightful scenery as any stream in Ulster'*. (McSkimin, 1831). The Belfast Water Commissioners acquired the surrounding lands in 1865 to construct reservoirs. A brick conduit nine miles long, fed the water to Belfast and a free daily allocation went to the town. The picturesque glen was improved by the commissioners with paths and steps so that the abundant ferns and other plants in the damp shady enclosures could be appreciated at close quarters.

ENTRANCE GATES TO GLYNN PARK HOUSE, 1920
(WAG 1080)

The impressive front entrance to Glynn Park with the crouching sphinx on each pillar was almost overwhelmed by the ornamental lamps of office, when William F. Coates was Lord Mayor of Belfast 1920-2. He received a Baronetcy during the Royal Visit of King George V and Queen Mary in June 1921. The pretty Victorian gate lodge is much later than the house and has survived, though the two sphinx have not.

LOVERS LANE *c.*1920 (WAG 1758)

Seen from the gates opposite, and looking toward North Road. Once the favourite walk for Carrick folk, especially courting couples, this has now been almost obliterated by bad planning. The walk divided here between a return to the town on the left or a continuation up Rocky Loanin'. The river, looking quietly rural at the stone bridge, had fed the bleachworks at Sullatober and a sluice gate further along, diverted the flow to Taylor's spinning mill.

71

DALWAY'S BAWN (WAG 1764)

Plantation families built substantial houses capable of being defended and with a walled yard or bawn to corral animals. This fine example at Bellahill was built by John Dallowaye in 1609 to secure a royal grant of land. Three out of four flanking turrets survive and the bawn remains part of a working farm though the dwelling has gone and also the overcoat of ivy. The turrets here were not solely defensive being spacious enough to provide living quarters for farmworkers.

BELLAHILL HOUSE, *c.*1920 (WAG 1761)

The Dalways soon became prominent in the district, serving as aldermen and members of parliament and built this fine house in 1794 to replace the nearby bawn as their home. The last member of the family to live here, Marriott Robert Dalway, left for Australia in the 1880s and in 1906 Egerton writes *'the* [mansion] *has been empty for some time and is falling into decay'*. The present owners bought the property in 1917 and removed the top storey in 1930 making its appearance today deceptively modern.

CARNMONEY, *c.* 1920 (WAG 3816)
Until quite recently Carnmoney was a rural village of one street ironically situated in the townland of Ballyduff and not Carnmoney. Although engulfed by suburban building the street remains recognizable. William Patterson's shop became Abernethy's in 1926 but retained this sign for many years and is now a car show room. The handsome house lost the bay window and became the post office. The Presbyterian Lecture Hall (1894) is on the left with the church out of sight behind.

74

CARNMONEY PARISH CHURCH (WAG 3813)

The Church of Ireland church is correctly in the townland of Carnmoney. Various churches occupied this site from early Christian times and the old graveyard predates the present church, built in 1856. The ground in front, sloping to the river became an extension of the graveyard in 1878 (distinguished by the yew trees). A Jewish graveyard is on the left where Tory Loanin' passed the church and ran on to present Whitewell Road. The mediaeval town of Coole here was burnt and destroyed by John de Logan in 1333, although the name persisted until the eighteenth century.

BALLYCLARE

Baile an clar: the settlement on the board, i.e. flat land. Ballyclare at the time when these photographs were taken, was a prosperous town of 2,000 inhabitants with plentiful employment in a variety of services and occupations in the town and the surrounding farms. The ford on the river was possibly the principal factor in the growth of the town, outstripping the neighbouring villages of Ballynure and Ballyeaston which in other respects appear to have had the same advantages.

Neolithic tools and early Christian church sites point to continuous human activity in the valley of the Sixmilewater from an early date, but there was little written evidence of Ballyclare until a Deed of Grant for Fairs and Markets was made to Lord Donegall in 1756 to regulate the increasing output of cloth and farm produce.

Cloth and paper had both been produced in the town prior to 1800 and, with technical advances, expanded greatly in the nineteenth century. This attracted the railway entrepreneurs and the town enjoyed the advantage of both broad and narrow gauge lines linking it to the ports of Larne and Belfast.

Observers varied in their accounts of Ballyclare. The Rev. John Dubourdieu in 1812 commented favourably that the people were *'in manner decent, in their conversation cheerful and for their station, well-informed.'* They were also *'acute at making bargains'* and *'frugal but not too parsimonious.'* The writer of the Ordnance Survey Memoir (1839) was not impressed. *'Ballyclare is built without the slightest regard to uniformity, regularity or neatness. It is anything but cleanly and its general appearance is uninteresting in the extreme'.* The more positive description given by Bassett's Guide and Directory 1888 sets the scene for life in the town shortly before it was photographed by Green. Although working hours were long and arduous, a sense of well-being showed in the range of entertainment and self-improvement enjoyed by the population. A reading society had 800 volumes and a newsroom. A lawn tennis club was quite advanced in allowing ladies to practice and play but not to be members. There was an annual sports day in August for the energetic, and also sixteen public houses which may seem excessive but was not unusual at that time.

Ballyclare is fortunate in having the works of a local writer living at this period, Archibald McIlroy, who used the town in thin disguise to set the scene for easily identifiable characters to act out stories often modelled on actual happenings. Accounts of everyday life in these old-fashioned novels are not only accurate in detail but in effect are vivid sketches illuminating the era as no text book of social history could.

The strong sense of local identity nurtured over the years by the self-sufficiency of the town was offended by incorporation in 1973 in the post-war creation, Newtownabbey. Ballyclare appeared a reluctant partner in a structure where the bulk of the population and most of the business lay elsewhere. Ballyclare continues within this alliance but has demonstrated its 'thrawn' nature by remaining essentially a county town and the revival of the famous May fair in 1983 has reinforced this insistence on going on its own way.

MARKET SQUARE, *c*. 1910 (WAG 851)

The wooden Market House on the fair green was replaced in 1858 by a stone building and an upper storey was added in 1873 to make a Town Hall. That building (seen here) was remodelled and enlarged in 1935. The weighbridge is in front and a gully known as 'the trinket' beyond. Along the side is the stone platform on which farm workers stood at the hiring fairs. The handsome memorial to Dr James Cunningham (1782-1853) was taken down in 1952.

'The Duke of York once crossed by air from London to Stranraer,
And on its route the royal plane passed over Ballyclare
On peeping out the Duke exclaimed, "Behold, the Court of Saul,"
"Och, nonsense", said the pilot, "that's Ballyclare Town Hall."'
Verse from poem by Sandy Robinson (of Ballyalbanagh) broadcast on B.B.C. at the time of opening of the new Town Hall) 23rd October 1935.

MAIN STREET, BALLYCLARE, LOOKING TOWARDS THE
SQUARE, *c.* 1910 (WAG 852)
The square was the heart beat of the town with frequent markets
and fairs and the Town Hall was occupied by meetings, dances
and concerts. Main Street was the spine of this compact town and
nine out of the ten shops advertising in Bassett's guide were here.
The buildings old and new look well kept and prosperous, in
keeping with the character of the town. The popular Hustie
Craig's Bar was replaced by the Ulster Bank in 1925. The Central
Dining Rooms next door remain. On the right is an unchanged
sexton's cottage next to the railings of the Old Presbyterian
Church.

MAIN STREET FROM THE SQUARE, *c.* 1910 (WAG 853)

On market and fair days, the throngs of people, animals, stalls and vehicles extended the length of Main Street from the square and were occasions for news, gossip and courting as well as business. The town seems unusually quiet in both photographs, with the camera providing interest for the few onlookers. At the telephone sign was Girvan's, another popular bar and opposite, Sam Cochrane has hung bicycle inner tubes to advertise, despite the dearth of customers.

DOAGH ROAD, BALLYCLARE, *c.* 1910 (WAG 856)
The fine Northern Bank (1868) is on the north-west corner of the square, beyond St John's Church of Ireland church on the right. The shop in the distance has gone, leaving the buildings behind open to the square. The R.I.C./R.U.C. barracks was to the left of that and the church beside J. Fleming's paint and wallpaper shop was Bethany Hall. The market handled so much pork that the line of carts waiting to use the weigh-bridge stretched from the square to this point and on occasion, beyond.

BALLYNURE ROAD, *c.* 1910 (WAG 858)
This sharp corner led to a small group of houses where the work force for the early paper mill lived. The gable and outbuildings belong to Millvale House, (contemporary with the old mill) where the manager lived. The site of the ponds and sluices lay to the left beyond the mill and has been cleared. Millvale House is being restored by the present owners.

OLD MILL, MILLVALE (WAG 864)

Paper was produced on this site from the early eighteenth century and at one time the business was owned by Francis Joy, the founder of the *Newsletter*. Production ceased in 1824 and the mill was later converted for corn. It never prospered as a corn mill and the site was taken over by the expanding bleachworks about 1900 to house beetling engines. Cheaper methods put an end to the mill in the 1920s although the bleachworks installed pumping machinery to continue making use of the water in the mill race. The ruins have since been removed.

NORTH OF IRELAND PAPERMILLS (WAG 861)
Paper making on this site expanded rapidly when a new company was formed in 1875 with English capital. The earlier stone buildings are out of sight behind the ambitious new development which eventually covered thirty-five acres and employed three hundred people. Most of the newspapers in Ireland used Ballyclare paper and the output of quality paper was especially notable. The business closed in 1950 and when the last chimney came down in 1989 a local historian wrote *'Let's not forget as it tumbles down that Ballyclare was Papertown.'* Jack McKinney

BLEACHWORKS, BALLYCLARE (WAG 860)

This huge concern started in the mid eighteenth century as a small family business. Expansion began in 1873 when John J. Kirkpatrick of Henryfield Farm took over and it continued as Kirkpatrick Bros after amalgamation in the Bleachers Association in 1900. The latest machinery was installed and it grew to become one of the biggest cloth finishers in the United Kingdom. The earlier mill buildings on the left have been cleared away. The green in foreground covered six acres and long linen strips were spread there until the 1940s. The firm now trades as *LINRON*.

SIXMILEWATER FROM THE TOWN BRIDGE (WAG 857)

The original name of the river, Ollar, meaning rushes in Irish, suggests a shallow widespread flow meandering along the valley bottom. The name changed when military dispatch riders between Carrickfergus and Antrim made a regular stop at a point upstream on the river, six miles from the castle. The bridge here in Main Street marks the early ford. The narrow-guage railway on the right also passed under Main Street and the railings are cattle pens. The footbridge served a path taking workers to the paper mill (see the chimney half hidden by the trees). The Methodist Church Hall is now on the left.

BALLYNURE, MAIN STREET, *c.* 1920 (WAG 751)

Traffic between Belfast and Larne has been diverted to a new road leaving the village as quiet as it appears here. The Presbyterian Church on the left was the scene of a local drama on 15th October 1797 when the minister arrived from Carrickfergus with the body of William Orr who had been executed for administering the oath of the United Irishmen. The body was waked all night by a packed congregation and many people afterwards wore rings inscribed 'Remember Orr'. The photographer's car makes a nice focal point.

BALLYNURE, *c.* 1920 (WAG 752)
This end of the village was known as Toberdowney as it was across the boundary of that townland. John McKinstry's shop, obviously a popular spot, was demolished about 1940. The fine two storey thatched building was Girvan's, a spirit grocer, and now a private dwelling. The modern name Castle Road refers to neighbouring Castleton where there had been a residence of the Dobbs family who owned the land.

ROUGHFORT RATH (WAG 98A)
Raths are the commonest field monument in Ireland and often called forts though their purpose was as farmsteads. The summit of this rath became a focal point in the community on 7th June 1798 when Henry Joy McCracken raised the banner of the United Irishmen there and marched off with several hundred local men singing the Marseillaise to attack the garrison at Antrim. It is recorded that only a few had muskets, most had hand made pikes and a lone cannon was hauled on a farm cart. Their high hopes ended in total rout.

CAIRNGRANNY DOLMEN (WAG 97)

This Neolithic chambered tomb, forty five feet long, is 300 yards from the rath in Craigarogan townland. The local name, Granny's grave is an amusing corruption of the Irish *greine* — sun which might refer to sun worship or simply a sunny position. The enclosing cairn has disappeared,as have two surrounding circles which were removed for agricultural improvement. (S. C. Lewis *Topographical Dictionary of Ireland*, London, 1838). H. C. Lawlor, P.R.I.A. excavated (1914-16) and found nine chambers with a cinerary urn and burnt human bone.

ROUGHFORT (WAG 71)

The hamlet is in the townland of Craigarogan and takes its name from the rath (page 88) which probably means 'red fort' for no apparent reason now. The simple almost primitive appearance of rural life could be misleading. Good land and productive farms meant a healthy though monotonous diet and strict religious observation and a high regard for education led to much talking and writing of a thoughtful nature. The Roughfort Book Club founded by local weavers in 1796 had a regular attendance of forty members and a stock of four hundred volumes. W. A. Green's Model T Ford has brought us safely to the end of this tour of East Antrim.

BIBLIOGRAPHY

County Antrim one hundred years ago: a guide and directory 1888, G. H. Bassett (Friar's Bush Press, 1989) is packed with well-informed accounts of all the towns and villages in the county at the end of the last century. The first *Shell Guide To Ireland* (London, 1962) is particularly detailed on history and architecture, and Richard Hayward's *In Praise of Ulster* (Belfast, 1936) is full of personal impressions and anecdotes. *Historic Monuments of N. Ireland*, (HMSO, Belfast, 1938) is a necessary handbook for exploring the countryside and *A Local Illustrated Historical and Antiquarian Guide for Tourists* compiled by the Rev. T. Egerton (Belfast, 1906) is a charming period piece. *Shadows On Glass* (Belfast, 1976) by Brian M. Walker has short biographies and representative photographs of the early photographers in Ulster.

Each district council produces a town guide and map (available from the council offices in Larne, Carrickfergus and Ballyclare) which has a brief history and notes on important sites in the area. The historical societies in Ballyclare and Carrickfergus, Larne Folklore Society and Islandmagee Conservation Society all produce printed material regularly.

The History of Newtownabbey (Antrim, 1979) by Robert Armstrong includes a section on Ballyclare and Jack McKinney covers more than the promised fairs and markets of the town in *They Came In Cars and Carts* (Antrim, 1989). The required reading for Carrickfergus is *M'Skimin's History of Carrickfergus*, new edition by E. J. M'Crum (Belfast, 1909) and No. 2 in the *Irish Historic Towns Atlas*, Carrickfergus by Philip Robinson (R.I.A. Dublin, 1986). The Ulster Architectural Heritage Society List No 23 — *Carrickfergus* (Belfast 1978) by Gordon Campbell and Susan Crowther gives historical information as well as architectural opinion and Sheela Speers also provides much background for her collection of photographs in *Under The Big Lamp* (Friar's Bush Press, Belfast, 1989). *Carrickfergus And It's Contacts* by John F. MacNeice (Belfast 1928) is good reading when it can be found. *The Carnmoney Connection* by Ernest V. Scott (Belfast, 1985) tells more than the stated history of the parish church. Dixon Donaldson's *History Of Islandmagee* (Carrickfergus, 1927) and Donald Akenson's *Between Two Revolutions* (Ontario, 1979) cover the island fully. A booklet *The Gobbins Cliff Path* by W. J. Fennell (Belfast, 1902) tells the story of that enterprise.

ACKNOWLEDGEMENTS

The Trustees of the Ulster Folk and Transport Museum kindly gave permission for photographs from the W. A. Green Collection to be reproduced here. Ken Anderson and the photographic department of the Museum produced the excellent prints.

My gratitude is due to Jack McKinney (Ballyclare), Ernie Scott (Ballynure) Mervyn McDowell (Carrickfergus), Trevor McGowan (Islandmagee), Maureen and Billy Close (Larne) and Paddy O'Donnell (Whitehead) who were kind enough to give time and thought to looking over my material. Jenny Brennan in Larne Historical Centre and Molly Coppock in Whitehead Library dug deep in the records for me, and my mother Roberta Luney tested her memory dating clothes. Joanne Robinson gave permission to quote from a poem by her uncle Sandy Robinson, Michael McCaughan and Eric McCleery assisted me greatly in the Ulster Folk and Transport Museum and the staff in the Linenhall Library were patient as ever. I would like finally to thank Brian Walker of Friar's Bush Press and especially Margaret McNulty who nursed me all the way.

The following photographs were not used but are available from the photographic department at the Ulster Folk and Transport Museum, Cultra, Co. Down.

88	Roughfort - earthen fort	855	Ballyclare - Doagh Road	2565	Larne - Antrim cliffs
96	Roughfort - chambered tomb	859	Ballyclare - bleachworks	2565A	Larne - Antrim cliffs
101	Carrickfergus - castle	862	Ballyclare - fort	2567	Gleno - waterfall
102	Carrickfergus - castle	863	Ballyclare - Craighill	2943	Whitehead
104	Gobbins - path	952	Islandmagee - Brown's Bay	2943A	Whitehead
105	Gobbins - Hillsport	954	Islandmagee - Brown's Bay	2944	Whitehead
106	Gobbins - cliff head	957	Dolmen - Ballylumford	3299	Carrickfergus - castle
107	Gobbins - oval girder bridge	1077	Carrickfergus - castle	3503	Whitehead - Black Head
110	The Laird rock	1078	Carrickfergus - castle	3504	Whitehead - Black Head
127	Dolmen in front of house, Ballylumford	1079	Carrickfergus - castle	3575	Whitehead - boulders
147	Larne - from shore, the Curran	1081	Carrickfergus - Glynn Park	3576	Whitehead - Black Head
301	Gleno	1082	Carrickfergus - Glynn Park	3589	Islandmagee- Kilcoan
303	Gleno - waterfall	1083	Whitehead - from cliff	3613	Larne
518	Gobbins - cliffs	1084	Whitehead - from cliff	3852	Carrickfergus - gaol
518A	Gobbins - cliffs	1085	Whitehead - from promenade	3856	Carrickfergus - King William's stone
519	Gobbins - cliff path	1086	Whitehead - Victoria Avenue	3857	The Round House, Kilroot
520	Gobbins - cliff head	1087	Whitehead - Marine Parade	3862	Whitehead
522	The Gobbins bridge	1090	Gobbins - tubular bridge		
523	The Gobbins bridge	1091	Gobbins - cliff head		
526	Larne Methodist Church	1100	Islandmagee		
531	Larne - Roman Catholic Church	1403	Islandmagee - Brown's Bay		
538	Larne - ladies bathing place	1462	Islandmagee - Port Muck		
541	Larne - cliff path	1751	Carrickfergus - castle		
542	Larne - Laharna Hotel	1753	Carrickfergus - castle		
543	Larne - Barnhill and Curran Road	1759	Carrickfergus - North Gate		
545	Larne - Cross Street and Town Hall	1762	Carrickfergus - Upper fall		
548	Larne - Prince's Gardens	2021	Gobbins - cliff head		
549	Larne - Clonlee	2022	Gobbins - from south		
758	Whitehead - town from south	2024	Gobbins - from path		
759	Whitehead - from the Banks	2024A	Gobbins - from path		
760	Whitehead - Cable Road	2076	Islandmagee - Brown's Bay		
763	Whitehead - Promenade	2076A	Islandmagee - Brown's Bay		
765	Whitehead - Marine Hotel	2163	Islandmagee - Mill Bay		
768	Whitehead - Balfour Avenue	2192	Larne - Black Cave tunnel		
770	Whitehead - Roman Catholic Church	2225	Larne - Antrim Coast		
771	Whitehead - Church of Ireland church	2558	Carrickfergus - castle		
772	Whitehead - cliff path	2558A	Carrickfergus - castle		
773	Black Head and lighthouse	2559	Carrickfergus - castle		
774	Black Head and the Gobbins	2562	Larne - Chaine monument		
854	Ballyclare - Doagh Road	2562A	Larne - Chaine monument		